The Dancers

Written by

Thomas Peacock

Illustrated by Jacqueline Paske Gill

To all our warriors

"Warriors aren't just those who go to war. Warriors are all the people who do good things.

They visit the sick. They hunt and fish and give food to the hungry.

They become mothers and fathers to children who are without parents."

~from The Forever Sky

Published by

Amazon On Demand Publishing LLC

ISBN: 9781093267365

Three summers ago when I was still a little kid, my mother and auntie took me to a powwow where we danced and danced.

Mother and Auntie were fancy shawl dancers. They danced like butterflies. Someday I hope to be as good a dancer as my mother and auntie.

That summer we spent a lot of time with my auntie. Then she joined the army. She left to become an ogichidaquay (female warrior).
The day she left, my mother and I sang her a traveling song when she got on the plane.

From that day on we prayed every day because we knew she might go to the war. And she did.

Auntie was in the war for many months. Then one morning my mother came to my room. She sat next to me on the bed and took my hand. She said Auntie was in a truck that drove over a bomb, which exploded. She said doctors were flying her to a hospital back in America.

I worried about Auntie a lot that day and all that followed.

She was in a faraway hospital a long time. There, the doctors and nurses worked hard to help her heal. Our community said prayers for her at our ceremonies.

Then after many months in hospital she was ready to fly home. We went to the airport to meet her. When the army nurse helped her from the plane I saw for the first time that the bomb had taken her legs.

I cried when I saw her like that in a wheelchair, but Auntie said, "No, my girl, be strong." So I pretended I was strong, just for her.

From that day on Auntie came and lived with us, my mother and me. Sometimes when she was in pain or having bad dreams I would go to her room and sing to her.

The seasons changed spring into summer, and my auntie and I became the best of friends. She taught me to be strong.

Then it was time again for a powwow. At first Auntie didn't want to go. "I don't want others to see me like this," she said, "And I can't dance anymore."

"No, Auntie, you can dance," I said. "You can dance with your heart." At first Auntie said no. But I said, "Auntie, please."

So she agreed to dance. As I helped push her from the car to the dance area, I saw how some people stared at her.

Soon the announcer asked the singers to do an honor song for the veterans. When the song began I asked Auntie if I could push her around the dance area in her wheelchair. Both my mother and I helped push Auntie that day.

She danced with her heart.

We had fun that weekend. I got to show Auntie how much better a dancer I was because I had been practicing.

We went to other powwows that summer. At each one my mother and I pushed Auntie around the dance area whenever an honor song was sung.

Then one day the Veteran's Hospital called. They said Auntie could be fitted with new legs and could learn to walk again. She was gone a long time and when she returned she could walk, slowly at first. Each week she got better.

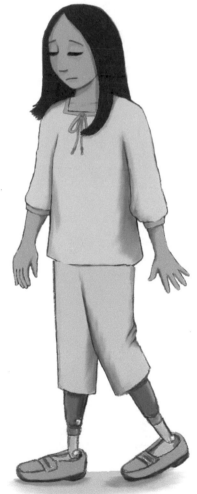

The seasons changed to fall, then to winter. That winter my mother and Auntie made jingle dress dance outfits, which are worn in the healing dance. And they made me a fancy shawl outfit.

I told Auntie that someday I hoped to be as good a dancer as she. I said to her, "I will dance because I want to honor you that way."

"My girl," Auntie said, "You taught me to dance again. You taught me to dance with my heart."

Soon it was summer again, and time for a powwow. When Auntie and Mother entered the dance area I could see everyone looking at them, especially Auntie. She danced so proud with her new legs. She held her head high. Most of the crowd was smiling and clapping when they saw Auntie dancing. Many were wiping away tears.

Later, I asked my mother why. My mother said Auntie is a hero, an ogichida. She went to war to help protect us and our way of life. And because of it she suffered the loss of her legs. She still sometimes has pain and bad dreams, but she is getting better. Now she can dance again. And dancing will help heal her even more.

My auntie. She risked her life so we can always live on this land among our people, free to be whom we are. Free to be strong. Free to dance with our hearts.

CPSIA information can be obtained
at www.ICGtesting.com
Printed in the USA
LVHW071712180120
644105LV00012B/274